Natural
Evangelism

THE PRACTICE OF PRAYING, CARING AND SHARING

J.JOHN

CONTENTS

FOREWORD

J.John is one of the Church's greatest communicators, blessed with gifts of teaching, humour, story-telling and integrity. *Natural Evangelism: The Practice of Praying, Caring and Sharing* is practical and packed full of stories, insights and activities to stimulate the Church into evangelistic action.

Evangelism is all about good news: good news for the poor, freedom for prisoners, sight for the blind, release for the oppressed, all of which proclaim the sovereign reign of God in the world today. For too long the Church has 'given up the turf' and withdrawn to the safety of church life, failing to proclaim this good news with confidence and conviction. As a consequence, our society is like a building shored-up with scaffolding but lacking firm foundations.

The current task of the Church is to reconnect imaginatively with the people of the twenty-first century. To do this, individual Christians need to communicate with confidence their own story of faith and understand how God's story still has the power to transform the lives of others in a similar way.

Taking seriously Jesus' command to go and make disciples of all nations, by word and deed, *Natural Evangelism* provides accessible and well-thought-out material to assist the Church in meeting that challenge.

J.John knows that terrain well. He is a practitioner and writes with many years of personal experience behind him. As someone responsible for encouraging the Church to think beyond its walls and to equip herself for the task of witness, I warmly commend *Natural Evangelism* and its author to you with confidence and the expectation that God will increase the gifts of faith and love in you as you play your part in sharing the Good News and thereby hasten the coming of God's kingdom of justice, peace and joy in the Holy Spirit. And remember: our Lord promised to be with us till the end of time and he gave us his authority and power.

The Most Revd Dr John Sentamu
Archbishop of York

1

THE **'WHY'** OF EVANGELISM

THE GREAT OMISSION?

At the end of Jesus' life on earth, he gave this charge to his followers:

> 'All authority in heaven and on earth has been given to me. Therefore go and make disciples of all nations, baptising them in the name of the Father and of the Son and of the Holy Spirit.' (Matthew 28:18–19)

Unfortunately, many of us are like Arctic rivers: frozen at the mouth. Most of us have missed opportunities to talk about Jesus with our relatives, friends, neighbours and work colleagues because we've 'frozen' on the spot.

But why do we freeze? If we had to share the Good News of Jesus with our friends what would hold us back? How might we approach the task creatively?

Now let's imagine ourselves in the position of a non-Christian friend. How would we react if we were engaged in a discussion about our beliefs? What would make us comfortable or uncomfortable in the way that we were approached?

Clearly, many of us have reservations and fears when it comes to evangelising. The Bible says, 'Fearing people is a dangerous trap' (Proverbs 29:25, NLT) – and this, for me, sums up our biggest fear: other people. Fear comes in many forms, but here are four common ones:

FEAR OF BEING INADEQUATE

We shouldn't be worried about what we do *not* know, but share what we *do* know. Jesus taught profound truths in very simple ways. He said, 'Unless you change and become like little children, you will never enter the kingdom of heaven' (Matthew 18:3). It's important for us to be confident about the Good News that we have to offer and not panic.

FEAR OF LOSING REPUTATION

We are often paralysed by what others will say or think of us. Yet the Bible says that Jesus 'made himself nothing' for us (Philippians 2:7). He is the example for us to follow. At Golgotha when Jesus was crucified, he had no reputation to lose. So why should we worry about ours?

However, that doesn't mean to say that we shouldn't present the message graciously, sensitively and with care.

FEAR OF REJECTION

Rejection is hard to handle, since we have a built-in need for love and acceptance.

FEAR OF APPEARING HYPOCRITICAL

Do our lives demonstrate the difference that the gospel makes? Or are we living so inconsistently, having succumbed to the attitudes and moral standards around us, that we are no longer credible?

Jesus made it clear that if we are going to follow him, we should not be surprised that some people will reject us. After all, he – of all people – was 'despised and rejected' (Isaiah 53:3). The Bible says that 'he came to his own people, and even they rejected him' (John 1:11, NLT).

The Greek word for witness is *'marturia'* – from which we derive the word 'martyr'. As the apostle Paul made clear to Timothy, 'everyone who wants to live a godly life in Christ Jesus will be persecuted' (2 Timothy 3:12).

Many did accept Jesus, many also rejected him. We shouldn't be surprised when we face rejection as it is part of the process of sharing the Good News of Jesus.

We are not told to provoke or invite rejection, but we are told to expect it.

THINK ABOUT

- How have people reacted when you have tried to share the Good News of Jesus?

- What works and what doesn't work?

- What lessons have you learned from your previous attempts?

WHAT IS EVANGELISM?

Sometimes within our culture, 'good' words can become 'bad' words, carrying negative connotations. Today, the verb 'to evangelise' – which is clearly biblical and appears 52 times in the New Testament – is looked upon with suspicion by many people who don't want religion shoved down their throats.

So what does 'evangelism' mean? Evangelism is the practice of sharing the gospel of Jesus Christ. The word 'gospel' means good news. To first-century followers of Christ, the 'gospel' was indeed news of 'victory over the enemy' made possible through Jesus Christ.

Evangelism is to pass on good news. William Temple, Archbishop of Canterbury during the Second World War, penned the following definition:

> To evangelise is to present Jesus Christ in the power of the Holy Spirit, that people may come to put their trust in God through him, to accept him as their Saviour and serve him as their King in the fellowship of the Church.
>
> William Temple
> *Towards the Conversion of England*

Let's remember that words mean nothing without actions. In Luke 4:18–19, we find Jesus in the synagogue reading from Isaiah 61:

> 'The Spirit of the Lord is on me, because he has anointed me to proclaim good news to the poor. He has sent me to proclaim freedom for the prisoners and recovery of sight for the blind, to set the oppressed free, to proclaim the year of the Lord's favour.'

It is evident from the passage above, and indeed the life of Christ, that the *proclamation* of the Good News (*words*) is only one side of the coin, the other being a *demonstration* of the Good News (*works*). We can't just throw words at people, however good the words are. Just as faith without works is dead, evangelism without godly action is hypocrisy.

THINK ABOUT

- Do we endeavour to 'practise what we preach'?

- Do we believe what we are trying to share with others?

- As we endeavour to be Natural Evangelists, how can we ensure that our conversations have integrity and authenticity?

WHY SHOULD WE EVANGELISE?

1. THE COMMAND OF CHRIST

Jesus gave us clear instructions to spread the Good News. He commanded us to 'go and make disciples'. This has become known as the 'Great Commission' (which can be found in Matthew 28:19–20):

> 'Therefore go and make disciples of all nations, baptising them in the name of the Father and of the Son and of the Holy Spirit, and teaching them to obey everything I have commanded you. And surely I am with you always, to the very end of the age.'

In this passage, we are told to do three things:

- to *make* disciples (people need to become committed to Jesus Christ)
- to *mark* disciples (baptising them)
- to *mature* disciples (helping them to grow in wisdom and faith).

Evangelism is not just about bringing people to a point of making a decision for Christ, it is also about helping them embark on a lifetime of obedience to Jesus.

2. THE ROLE OF THE CHURCH

A church that does not do its best to help others to become Christians is disobedient and guilty of the sin of omission. Jesus said, 'All who love me will do what I say' (John 14:23, NLT).

The Church is about three things:

i. Looking up – worship

Worship is celebrating the presence of God over his creation and among his people. It includes our response in adoration, confession and a desire to encounter his power, truth and beauty. True worship is inwardly transforming and outward in focus, as we share God's compassion for a world in desperate need of him.

ii. Looking in – well-being

Well-being is the closest we can get in English to translating the Hebrew word 'shalom' – peace. It signifies a balanced life that is blessed by God. It cannot be experienced in isolation but flows from relationships that are accepting, affirming, accountable and transforming. These relationships provide the context in which we can grow into our God-given potential and contribute to the ministry of the whole church, both within the believing community and to the needs of the surrounding community and the world.

iii. Looking out – witness

Witness is our first-hand testimony in both words and actions. We are witnesses to what God has done *for* us in Christ through the sacrifice of his Son on the cross, to what Christ continues to do *in* us through his Spirit to make us more like himself, as well as to what he achieves *through* us to continue his ministry in the world.

Do you and your church have an equal balance of these three categories: worship, well-being and witness?

3. THE COMPASSION OF CHRIST

If we really love God, we will love other people. Jesus was deeply moved by human needs. In Matthew 9:36–38 we read:

> When he saw the crowds, he had compassion on them, because they were harassed and helpless, like sheep without a shepherd.

Then he said to his disciples, 'The harvest is plentiful but the workers are few. Ask the Lord of the harvest, therefore, to send out workers into his harvest field.'

In the original Greek, 'compassion' is a very strong word, full of deep, gut-level feeling and emotion. It's about being moved to the depths of one's heart, 'suffering with someone' by entering into their despair and pain.

Evangelism is not just about numbers; we count people because people count. Because we are made in the image of God, every individual is a person of intrinsic worth.

4. THE CONVICTION OF CHRIST

The Church is a living organism, and all living things grow. Jesus was committed to the growth of his Church. 'Jesus went through all the towns and villages, teaching in their synagogues, proclaiming the good news of the kingdom and healing every disease and illness' (Matthew 9:35). We see here that Jesus used words, works and wonders to expand the kingdom.

Jesus also said, 'I will build my church' (Matthew 16:18); it is his Church and he wants it to grow. Many of his parables use growth terminology and imagery.

What's more, the New Testament demonstrates numerical growth. At the start of the book of Acts, we read that the number of disciples was around 120. Towards the end of the book, as the disciples had spread the Word, they numbered 'many thousands' (Acts 21:20). That is serious growth! But the growth Jesus has in mind results not just in bigger crowds of believers, but also in people being transformed by the gospel of the kingdom, so that they make a difference in their communities and in society at large.

5. THE CONSUMMATION OF CHRIST'S KINGDOM

Jesus said, 'This gospel of the kingdom will be preached in the whole world as a testimony to all nations, and then the end will come' (Matthew 24:14).

One of the prerequisites of Christ's return is the spread of the Christian message to the whole world. The Bible does not say that there will be world conversion before Christ returns, but it does say there will be world *evangelisation*. Everyone must hear, although not everyone will respond.

As the world's population increases, the task gets harder. At the time of the Great Commission, the world population was about 170 million. Today it is around 7 billion. There are now 196 nations and 271 major languages.

Many of us have heard opportunity knocking at our door but, as someone once said, by the time we unhooked the chain, pushed back the bolt, turned two locks and switched off the burglar alarm, it was gone. We are all faced with great opportunities, brilliantly disguised as impossible situations. Our response is so often too little, too late. The knock on the door is simply ignored or goes unheeded because we are too preoccupied with our own agendas.

THINK ABOUT

- How many of your relatives, friends, neighbours or work colleagues know about the treasure you possess?

- How infectious is your love of Jesus?

- If you have forgotten that Jesus is your most precious treasure, how can you help to remind yourself of the wonderful gift you have received?

SEEING THE BIG PICTURE

It's even harder to evangelise others when we ourselves don't fully grasp the Good News we're called to share. If we are to be effective communicators, it is crucial to remind ourselves continually of the Good News itself – and to establish, in our mind's eye, the 'bigger picture' of our faith and where we fit into it.

To communicate the optimism and hope of the gospel, we need to be able to explain the big picture of God's positive attitude and dealings with humanity throughout history. The whole sweep of God's story is presented to us in the Old and New Testaments, and there is no substitute for reading through the whole Bible from start to finish to understand this better. Just reading the Bible for 15 minutes a day will enable you to read through the Bible in a year.

In Ephesians 1:3 – 2:13, Paul provides us with a helpful snapshot summary of that history. Read this passage in your Bible before continuing.

We can break this passage into six sections (see Appendix 1 for Bible references):

1. Creation (the relationship between God and humanity).

2. Chaos (sin and separation).

3. Covenant (covenant blessing and promise – Abraham).

4. Christ the Mediator.

5. Christ the Conqueror (Jesus rises from the dead).

6. Certainty (new life by the Spirit and our inheritance assured).

THINK ABOUT

- How would you summarise the big picture to communicate it to someone else?

- Who took the initiative to mend the relationship between God and humankind?

- Think about those who are not (or not yet) Christians. What does the passage say about their present relationship to God and their future?

- Think about those who are believers in Christ. What does the passage say about their present relationship with God and their future?

- How does knowing and understanding the big picture help us in sharing our faith?

A PRAYER

Father, Son and Holy Spirit, Creator, Redeemer and Comforter, thank you that you work in perfect harmony as you create and sustain our world and the universe. Forgive us when we neglect to spread the message that you are Good News. May your perfect love cast out all our fear. Please help us to encourage each other, as we reflect on the wonderful treasure you have given us – forgiveness for the past, new life for today and a hope for the future. We want to pass on this Good News. Please inspire us to be creative, courageous communicators of the gospel. Amen.

2

WHAT IS THE **GOOD NEWS** OF CHRISTIANITY?

GETTING THE MESSAGE RIGHT

If we don't explain a message clearly, it can have disastrous consequences! Take the story of a couple travelling through Asia with their much-loved pet dog. When they entered one town they found a restaurant and, with the aid of gestures and a phrase book, they persuaded the waiter to take the dog away and feed him.

Imagine how they felt, therefore, when their beloved dog was presented to them, grilled and neatly served on a plate. They had communicated a message – but it was the wrong one!

We have all been the victims and the perpetrators of miscommunication. It can happen in so many different ways. Have you had an experience when you've tried to say one thing but have been understood in a completely different way altogether? What did you learn from the experience?

Sometimes we fail to get the message because we have stopped listening while the other person is speaking! We might like to reflect on how well we listen to others.

WHAT IS A CHRISTIAN?

Before we really begin to be Natural Evangelists and to share the Good News, it is vital to ask ourselves, 'What is a Christian?'

What is it that marks us out as different? Contemplate how to define what a Christian is and how to sum that up to someone in a few words.

GOD-TALK: ARE THEY THINKING WHAT YOU'RE THINKING?

When we talk to people about God, we might assume that we share the same understanding of the character and personality of God. Yet people outside (and sometimes even within) the Christian faith may have a very different way of thinking about God – and we should be aware of that when we start any conversation.

THINK ABOUT

- In what ways has your own understanding of God changed since you became a follower of Christ?

- Have you ever stopped to think that your perception of God might be different from other people's?

- How might this affect the way you try to talk about God with others?

It's not just a case of whether a person believes in God – but what sort of God they believe in.

It's hard to define God on one level. After all, God is a mystery to be encountered and experienced, not a problem to be solved. God cannot be boxed into the narrow confines of our expectations.

The God of the Bible is a mystery that has been made known. We can't know everything there is to know about God, but we can know him and grow in our knowledge of him.

The word 'mystery' in the Bible conveys something we could never fathom, unless God makes it known. Look up Romans 16:25–26 and Colossians 1:26.

Many popular concepts of God are wrong because they are based on what individuals would like to believe God is like, or a notion of God that they reject, rather than what he is actually like. To paraphrase the great thinker Blaise Pascal, God created man in his own image and man has been returning the compliment ever since!

The renowned North American sociologist Robert N. Bellah conducted a survey asking people what they thought God was like. One woman called Sheila responded like this:

> God is so loving; he would never judge anyone. God doesn't require people to go to church. God doesn't expect people to live moral lives.

Bellah concluded that this woman was not a Christian, but a 'Sheilaist' as she had created a religion based purely on her own subjective opinions.

It is sometimes tempting to miss out certain aspects of God's character to make God sound more marketable. It is easier to sell the idea of a 'nice' God to someone, rather than a God of judgement. But we are neither in the business of selling or of making people 'feel' good. Instead we are trying to convey the true message that God himself has revealed who he is in Christ, how he relates to the world he has created and sustains, and how we can know him – overcoming the alienation caused by our wilful disobedience and waywardness.

THE GOSPEL IN A NUTSHELL

The 'Good News' that we want to share with people can be summed up in four simple statements. These don't cover every single nuance of the entire biblical sweep of history. However, if you're sitting on a train or talking to a neighbour, you won't always have time to explain everything in the finest detail! The following summary points should help you communicate the message in a short, succinct way, as you try to talk with others about God.

THE FOUR DS

Here are the statements:

1. God formed us: Design

In the first book of the Bible, Genesis (Hebrew for 'beginnings'), we are told, 'God created mankind in his own image . . . and it was very good' (Genesis 1:27–31).

God the Creator formed us as the crown and pinnacle of his creation – in his likeness.

2. Sin deformed us: Disorder

God's good creation did not stay that way for long and Genesis 3 records the story of the advent of sin into the world.

Notice that God gave Adam and Eve *general permission*: 'You are free to eat from any tree in the garden' (2:16) and *singular prohibition*: 'But you must not eat from the tree of the knowledge of good and evil' (2:17).

Adam and Eve chose to rebel against God's one prohibition (3:6) and sin contaminated the world like a virus infects a computer and brings disorder and chaos.

It is likely we can all testify to having had an Eden experience and then rebelling against God's good governance, straying from his presence. After all, sin has been defined as 'a three-letter word with "I" in the middle'!

The Bible account tells us that Adam and Eve's disobedience caused them to be excluded from the garden. In other words, it resulted in their alienation. They had to suffer the consequences of their attitudes and actions. We live with those consequences today.

3. Christ transforms us: Deliverance

Since the earliest of times, the serpent in the Eden story has been understood to represent the devil, who led humankind in rebellion against God. At the end of the account, God promises the serpent that a descendant of Eve 'will crush your head' (Genesis 3:15).

Thousands of years later, the apostle Paul declared that Jesus Christ 'disarmed the powers and authorities . . . made a public spectacle of them, triumphing over them by the cross' (Colossians 2:15).

The cross of Christ is God's great act of rescue. 'Jesus' literally means 'God saves' or a modern paraphrase would be 'God-to-the-rescue'. God has come to our rescue in Christ, delivering us from disorder and death through Christ's blood shed on the cross. His resurrection from the dead and subsequent ascension into heaven declares his victory over sin and death.

4. Scripture informs us: Decision

In John's Gospel we read, 'To all who did *receive* him, to those who *believed* in his name, he gave the right to become children of God' (John 1:12, emphasis mine).

Each of us has a decision to make. To decide to become a Christian is to:

* *Believe* in Jesus Christ and his message, repenting of our sins and placing our confidence in him.

* *Receive* Jesus Christ into our life by God's Holy Spirit who strengthens us to validate our faith in thought, word and deed.

* *Follow* Jesus Christ in every area of our life, for we are now part of his new creation and belong to his family.

WE BELIEVE . . .

The Church spent several hundred years debating the key elements of 'doctrine', so as to avoid false teaching and heresy. Finally, at the Council of Nicea in AD 325 (some of you may have grown up with the designation CE [Common Era] and may not recognise the Latin-rooted AD), the Early Church leaders agreed on the following description of our faith, known as the Nicene Creed. To conclude, and to remind us of what we believe, read the Creed:

We believe in one God,
The Father, the Almighty,
Maker of heaven and earth,
Of all that is, seen and unseen.
We believe in one Lord, Jesus Christ,
The only Son of God,
Eternally begotten of the Father,
God from God, Light from Light,
True God from true God,
Begotten, not made,
Of one Being with the Father;

Through him, all things were made.
For us and for our salvation he came down from heaven,
By the power of the Holy Spirit
Was incarnate from the Holy Spirit and the Virgin Mary
And was made man.
For our sake he was crucified under Pontius Pilate;
He suffered death and was buried.
On the third day he rose again
In accordance with the Scriptures;
He ascended into heaven
And is seated at the right hand of the Father.
He will come again in glory to judge the living and the dead,
And his kingdom will have no end.
We believe in the Holy Spirit,
The Lord, the giver of life,
Who proceeds from the Father and the Son,
Who with the Father and the Son is worshipped and glorified,
Who has spoken through the prophets.
We believe in one holy catholic and apostolic Church.
We acknowledge one baptism for the forgiveness of sins.
We look for the resurrection of the dead,
And the life of the world to come.
Amen.

A PRAYER

Creator God, thank you that you have designed each one of us. Even in our rebellion, you reached out to deliver us from the disorder caused by our sin.

Empower us by your Spirit, that we might have strength, courage and clarity of thought to communicate the transforming message of your gospel compassionately and effectively. Amen.

3

WHAT IS
FRIENDSHIP EVANGELISM?

EVANGELISM BEGINS AT HOME!

The book of Acts records the story of how the 'Good News' began to spread, opening the first chapter with the words of Jesus: 'You will receive power when the Holy Spirit comes on you; and you will be my witnesses in Jerusalem, and in all Judea and Samaria, and to the ends of the earth' (Acts 1:8).

That sounds quite frightening. How can we go to the ends of the earth and spread the gospel? Jesus told the disciples to start in Jerusalem, precisely because *that was where they were.* Jerusalem was where they had all deserted Jesus before he was crucified; one of their bleakest moments. It was also the place where they felt most threatened and where they wanted to conceal their presence. Jerusalem went on to become the starting point for their global mission. The Word would not spread to the ends of the earth unless it started where they were – at home – and this was their first and toughest challenge! No wonder they needed the message of assurance that they would receive the power of the Holy Spirit in Jerusalem to witness to Jesus.

So what does 'Jerusalem' mean to us? It is symbolic of our home – our immediate family, friends, neighbours and work colleagues. As it was for the disciples, it might also be the place of our greatest failings and fears. But unless we start there – in Jerusalem – our own mission to spread the Good News will never get off the ground.

In Acts 20:20, the Bible tells us that the gospel – the Good News – spread 'from house to house'. It should, likewise, go from our home to the homes of others we already know.

Historical note: we must recognise that 'house' in the New Testament refers to the household of a pre-industrial city. Before factories and offices, nearly all business and trade was undertaken in and from the home. So the house signified much more than a domestic family; it was a basic economic unit of society. Associated with the typical 'house' would be servants, clientele (customers) and the friends of the family. About 80 per cent of the working population consisted of labourers. The gospel spread in the early centuries from household to household, an interconnected network of relationships.

Who is in your 'Jerusalem'?

The Bible records many accounts of people encountering Christ or hearing the Good News whose response was to immediately go and share it with others.

Spend a few moments looking up the following verses. After reading each verse, pause for a moment and imagine that you are in the shoes of the person featured. Ask yourself, how do you think each person felt? What prompted their response? Why did they go and tell the people they told?

1. John 1:41–42: Andrew brought his *brother*.
2. John 1:43–45: Philip told his *friend Nathanael*.
3. John 4:28–30: The Samaritan woman told the *people in her town*.
4. Luke 5:27–32: Levi invited his *colleagues*.
5. Acts 16:25–34: The Philippian jailer shared with his *family*.

There are three natural groups of people within our 'Jerusalem'. It's important for us to identify them:

1. **Kin** (our family and close friends).

2. **Community** (those we meet regularly, such as work colleagues, our neighbours, school teachers).

3. **Interest** (those we share the same meeting place with, such as the golf club, gym or toddler group).

We're going to focus on 'Jerusalem' here, because that's where we have to start. But as we develop our skills at friendship evangelism, they should not be restricted to individuals we already know. A true witness must also ask regularly, 'To whom can I be a friend?' Then we'll begin to have the confidence to spread the word into 'Judea' and 'Samaria' – the friends and contacts we don't see so often, followed by those who we know but don't get on with – and then to 'the ends of the earth' (those people we've never even met).

It's time to identify those in our 'Jerusalem' who we haven't yet told about the Good News of Jesus Christ. If you keep a journal spend a few minutes writing down the names of those people you know well, who you haven't told about Jesus. Write down the name of the person in the relevant 'Jerusalem' – Kin, Community or Interest. If a person falls into more than one category, you can write their name in each column.

Ask the Lord to guide you to two people in each category and share their names with another Christian. Covenant to pray for them at least once a week. Hold each other accountable and provide encouragement in the coming days and weeks by recording the ways in which your prayers are being answered.

BUBBLING OVER!

Michael Marshall states that evangelism will happen naturally when the Church is at 'apostolic bubbling point'. What he means is that the best evangelism is not driven by feelings of guilt or duty, but is a natural by-product of falling deeply in love with Jesus. It is, quite simply, the overflow of the abundant life that Christ has made available to us. It is very difficult to get half-full Christians to overflow!

A missionary is not someone who crosses the sea; a missionary is someone who sees the cross. When we have encountered the love of Christ, his love compels us.

Whether we go a thousand miles or a hundred yards – the most difficult part of the journey is the last three feet!

Friendship evangelism is no ordinary exercise, no mundane task which we're obliged, out of duty, to tackle. Instead, it is driven by the twin values of compassion and love. Take Bob Geldof. When he saw on the news that millions of people in Ethiopia were starving to death, he didn't sit back and leave the problem to someone else. He did something about it and organised Live Aid and Live 8. He felt compassion and turned it into positive action.

Like Geldof, one of Jesus' main attributes was compassion for the people he met. He didn't see them as statistics (do we?). Instead, he saw their needs, felt their pain, shared their joy, and wanted to see their lives transformed for good.

Jesus doesn't call you to make disciples because he wants to give you a tough or embarrassing task to earn your place in heaven. Instead, he asks you to continue his work – which was birthed from the start by a very practical love. If we love God and our neighbour as the Bible calls us to, then the natural overflow of that love will be to introduce our neighbours to the God we love.

There are some things in life we just can't help talking about. If you've had a child, you'll know how hard it is not to talk about the good news of your new arrival. (And as they continue to grow, you'll find it hard not to keep boasting to your friends and relatives of their progress!) If you've ever fallen in love, you'll know how hard it is to contain your excitement: your natural reaction is to tell others how wonderful your boyfriend or girlfriend is – it's an overflow of your heart. You can't keep it in. Similarly, if your sports team wins the league, the cup, or even just a match, it's natural to share your delight with others. If you support a winning team, everyone knows – but does everyone know you're on God's side?

In Acts 4:20 (NLT), when the religious leaders told Peter and John to stop talking publicly about Jesus, Peter replied, 'We cannot stop telling about everything we have seen and heard.' They couldn't help themselves!

When it comes to evangelism, you can't give away what you haven't got!

You and I need to walk in intimacy with God, our hearts ablaze with the love of Christ. Then we will find that evangelism happens naturally as a by-product – an overflow of our burning hearts.

THINK ABOUT

- What things do you get excited about and can't stop talking about?

- Why do you get so excited about these things?

- Why can't you stop talking about them?

- Every day we communicate some message or other. Replay in your mind some conversations you've had in the last few days. Have you been a carrier of gossip or negative thoughts, or of good news?

TURNING THOUGHTS INTO ACTION

Have you ever stopped to wonder why people who aren't yet Christians come to church? I once read some fascinating statistics:

- 1 per cent come because they were visited by Christians.

- 2 per cent come because of the church programme – they've come along to a holiday club, a senior citizens' lunch, toddler group, and so on.

- 3 per cent come because of bereavement.

- 3 per cent come because of Sunday school.

- 6 per cent walk through the door because they see some publicity.

- 8 per cent come because of some personal contact they've had with the minister or church staff.

- And 77 per cent come because friends or relatives invited them.

It's easy enough to read statistics, but this one is worth stopping to think about for a moment: 77 per cent of people come to church because friends or relatives invite them. Have you contributed to this statistic?

We also have to acknowledge the fact that the problem may be that my church isn't the kind of place I would want to invite any of my friends to visit. What changes would need to take place before I felt confident that my friends would be likely to have a positive experience?

BREAKING DOWN THE BARRIERS BETWEEN US

Remember that you can't fish from a pond in which there are no fish. If we spend all our time with other Christians, we won't be in a position to invite people along to church in the first place. But even if we don't spend lots of leisure time with those who are not yet Christians, we'll have seen from the list of names we wrote down in our 'Jerusalem' that we come into contact with many people in our everyday lives with whom we can, if we have the courage, share the Good News.

Sometimes we think that the barriers between them and us are so great that we can't possibly talk about our faith. Yet Jesus showed us that barriers aren't always as great as they first appear. And every barrier you face is, after all, also a potential opportunity.

In John 4, we read the story of Jesus and the woman at the well. Jesus was faced with four barriers when he stopped to talk to her:

1. A moral barrier (she had committed adultery in the eyes of a Jew by taking several husbands).

2. A social barrier (she was a woman; he was a man).

3. A racial barrier (she was a Samaritan and Jesus a Jew, and the two ethnic groups despised each other).

4. A religious barrier (Jews and Samaritans didn't mix on religious grounds).

Yet Jesus addressed her at her point of need, which was greater than the supposed barriers: she was thirsty for living water and he cared enough to break the social taboo and offer it to her. You can trace the way Jesus cut through the barriers, as they spoke and she responded. First, she addressed him as 'Jew'; then, she called Jesus 'Sir'; then, she called him 'prophet'. Finally, she spoke of him as the 'Messiah'.

And as she responded to Jesus with her heart, she couldn't help but tell others the Good News, even though she simply raised a question, 'Come, see a man who told me everything I've ever done. Could this be the Messiah?' (John 4:29). The Bible records, 'Many of the Samaritans from that town believed in him because of the woman's testimony, "He told me everything I've ever done"' (John 4:39). Her experience provided her with the opportunity to raise the important question.

Jesus was the friend of sinners, and we need to learn from this. He was comfortable with those who didn't know God, and they with him – which I think is remarkable. But he wasn't just hanging out having a friendly chat. His friendship compelled him to help them change the way they lived. Jesus even lovingly pointed out to an older, respectable man, Nicodemus, that he was ignorant of 'heavenly things' (John 3:12).

If we are true friends, we will speak the truth in love.

SO WHERE DO WE START?

The key point is this: how can I care about someone and not share the most important fact in my life? Remember, we are not to preach at them. We are not to give a sermon, but to plant seeds of the grace of God. If we do this generously, the Bible says God is able to water the seed and make it grow.

Think for a few moments about who you could invite around to your home for a drinks evening. Perhaps it's the people on your 'Jerusalem' lists. It may, on the other hand, be your next-door neighbours – three to the left, three to the right and those opposite. Remember, the gospel spread originally 'from house to house'.

You could plan to do this at a special occasion such as Easter or Christmas. And there's no pressure to force the gospel down their throats in one go – instead, use the time to get to know them better and genuinely be interested in who they are and what makes them tick.

Simply be prepared to sow one seed: perhaps by giving them an invitation to a carol service or giving them a copy of a giveaway booklet as a gift. A girl became a Christian through a very timid and shy Christian. At her baptism, she shared her testimony and said, 'My friend built a bridge from her life to mine – and Christ walked over it.'

SOWING GENEROUSLY

It's crucial as we set about trying to tell people about the overflow of our heart – the Good News of Jesus – that we don't try to overfeed them. You wouldn't try to feed a leg of chicken to a baby. Instead, you'd take some of the meat, liquidise it and feed it in tiny spoonfuls.

Our job is to sow; God will produce the crop. We must not forget that ultimately God is the evangelist. We are called to serve faithfully, not succeed by forcing the issue.

Remember to be interested in the people you're talking to. Have a listening ear to where they are at and what they are really trying to say. They might say, 'I used to go to Sunday school,' 'I was married in church,' or 'Things have been hard since my mum died.' Don't be afraid to ask what they believe and what involvement they have had with the Christian faith.

A PRAYER

Gracious God, thank you for our friends, relatives, work colleagues and acquaintances. Thank you for all the good things they bring to our lives. Thank you for who they are and for who you have created them to be and to become.

Send your Holy Spirit upon us and set our hearts ablaze with love for you, that we might see them through your eyes – with love and compassion. And help us to see afresh the wonderful news that we have for them, that, through Jesus, we have a way back to you. Empower us afresh, that we might minister from the overflow of our hearts.

Please help us to start at home, in our own Jerusalem, by taking the courage to sow seeds of grace in the lives of the people we meet. We pray that you water those seeds through your Spirit and that we might all become like the disciples in those first, daunting days, who stepped out in faith to spread the word that the Messiah has died for us all, so that we all might live. In Jesus' name. Amen.

4

THIS IS **MY STORY**

WE MAY NOT BE EXPERTS, BUT WE ALL HAVE A STORY TO TELL

In today's culture, we like to look for an expert to help us on any given subject. So if, for instance, you're expecting a child, you will seek the advice of a midwife to help you prepare for the birth and subsequent care of your child. However, you'll still ask for advice from your family and friends who have already had a baby – and these people will often share some really useful stories that the midwife, despite her expertise, hasn't told you. Both the expert's information and the friends' anecdotal accounts have a vital role to play in painting a fuller picture.

When we come to sharing our faith, we might think we don't have all the facts and we're not 'expert' enough to break the news about Jesus to other people. It's very easy to focus so hard on what we *don't* know that we forget what we *do* know.

However, we're all very likely to have some wonderful things to say, including stories about the way God works that are unique to us. Our own stories about the role of God in our lives have a key part to play in spreading the gospel from home to home. They are real, personal and rooted in everyday life. They don't come from a textbook but from the heart, and this is often far more likely to speak to someone than a dry and well-rehearsed 'argument'.

Remember, when it comes to telling your story, *you* are the expert!

Don't forget that evangelism is essentially about introducing one person to another and, for that, you need the personal touch. You can win arguments and lose hearts and you can lose arguments and win hearts. The great thing about 'sharing our story' is that it is a form of evangelism which is very difficult to argue with.

'Jesus Christ has transformed my life' is not a proposition to be disproved but a statement of faith to be experienced. God entrusted the very first task of spreading the Good News not to university professors but to fishermen.

As we begin to think about how to tell our own stories, it's important to remember that you won't always be able to offer an answer. But that's OK. You will never know it all and people are usually happy to accept that we don't (in fact, it's a far more honest approach). That said, we mustn't be afraid to do some research. After all, to grow and develop in any new skill we need to be prepared to undergo some training, much the same as we do when we take lessons to learn to drive a car, ski down a mountain or play the piano.

THINK ABOUT

Jesus didn't always 'preach' to people. Instead, he identified their need and often either asked a question or told a story in response. Spend a few minutes looking through your Bible at some of the stories Jesus told. Choose one that speaks to you.

- To whom was Jesus telling the story?

- What kind of 'props' did he use – characters, plot, description?

- What was the listener's response, if it is recorded?

- Why does this story speak to you?

TELLING OUR STORY

The Good News of the gospel needs to be communicated in three parts:

1. **His story:** God's story from the beginning of creation through to the life, death and resurrection of Jesus.

2. **Your story:** how God's power came into your life and how this has changed and continues to change you.

3. **Their story:** how God's story relates to the person to whom you are witnessing.

The history of the world is ultimately God's story. When we realise this and that our story (or that of a friend) intersects with God's story, we truly find ourselves in HIStory – the only 'history' that will endure for eternity. (Theologians call this 'salvation history'.)

For the rest of this chapter, we'll focus on your story. Psalm 66:16 says, 'Come and hear, all you who fear God; let me tell you what he has done for me.' When Jesus healed the blind man in John 9, the man said, 'One thing I do know. I was blind but now I see!' (v.25).

There is the remarkable conclusion to the story of the demon-possessed man who, after Jesus had healed him, begged to be allowed to go with him. But Jesus instructed him, 'Go home to your own people and tell them how much the Lord has done for you, and how he has had mercy on you' (Mark 5:19). His witness was likely to be most effective among the people who knew him best. And in Acts 4:20, Peter tells the religious leaders who are trying to keep him quiet, 'We cannot help speaking about what we have seen and heard.'

Winston Churchill once remarked, 'Men occasionally stumble over the truth, but most pick themselves up and hurry off as if nothing had happened.' The experience of those biblical characters was very different – they had an encounter with the Creator of the cosmos and could not keep quiet. If we have met the same Creator God, we, too, will not be able to keep quiet. In these verses, we find several people who had met with God and couldn't help telling others the story of what happened.

We're *all* called to be witnesses for Jesus – but there's a difference between a witness and a lawyer. A witness simply tells the court what they have experienced. A lawyer, on the other hand, has to plead the case. An 'evangelist' is a bit like a lawyer – but not all of us are called to do this specific task. However, we *are* all called to give an account of what we have seen, heard and experienced of God.

WHY DO PEOPLE RECEIVE CHRIST?

Most of us receive Christ because of conviction, curiosity or crisis. With either our minds or with our hearts, we realise that we need him. Some of us have simply needed to hang around with Christians to observe and learn about Christ, before we are ready to receive him. It is the same with stories of how people came to marry their partner. With some it was love at first sight, whereas other couples knew each other for a while before they realised the love that had grown between them. It's useful to stop to think about what makes people realise they need Jesus. For some, it's loneliness. To all the lonely people in the world, Jesus offers friendship and love.

DIFFERENT KINDS OF TRANSFORMATION STORIES

The tradition of testimony – telling our story of encountering Christ – is as old as the Church itself. When the apostle Paul wrote to the Galatians, he did just this (Galatians 1:13–24). On this occasion, Paul's story had three sections:

1. His life before he encountered Christ

> You have heard of my previous way of life . . . how intensely I persecuted the church of God . . . (v.13)

2. How he encountered Christ

> . . . God, who set me apart from my mother's womb . . . was pleased to reveal his Son in me (v.15–16)

3. His transformation stories since encountering Christ

> The churches . . . heard the report: 'The man who formerly persecuted us is now preaching the faith he once tried to destroy.' (v.22–23)

We all have different kinds of transformation stories to tell. And while it's good to get the story right about our conversion, it's important to remember that each time God answers our prayers and does something new in our lives we have another story to tell.

Your story may not be as sudden and dramatic as that of the apostle Paul. Some people cannot remember a time when they did not love Jesus. For other people, their conversion was a gradual falling in love with Jesus. They cannot remember a specific place and time. If this has been your experience, don't assume that you do not have a testimony to the transforming power of Christ.

Like Paul's testimony, our story should be clear and have distinct sections. If you do not have a dramatic conversion story, your testimony might focus on the influences that led you to Christ and nurtured you, perhaps from a young age. You can record the moments of revelation and realisation of growing in understanding of what Christ did for you on the cross and the life to which he called you by the prompting and empowering of the Holy Spirit. A good way to look at it is to break our personal story into three categories:

1. My life before I encountered Christ.
2. How I encountered Christ.
3. My life since I encountered Christ.

Let's look at each one in turn. Begin to think, as we go through the three areas, of your own story and how it fits into these categories.

1. MY LIFE BEFORE I ENCOUNTERED CHRIST

We don't all need a 'conversion date' to prove we are Christians. After all, I can't remember the day I was born, but I was – and there seems to be evidence to support it!

However your conversion happened, you should give some thought to what your life was like before you followed Christ. How did you act? What were you like as a person? How did you approach life?

2. HOW I ENCOUNTERED CHRIST

Where and when did you start your relationship with Jesus? Was it sudden or gradual? (Don't forget, both are equally valid – so don't be tempted to manipulate your story to make it sound more dramatic. It will resonate with other 'normal people' precisely because it is real, not sensational.) What exactly did you do to become a Christian?

Was there an individual or a number of Christians whose lives made Jesus attractive to you and what was appealing about their invitation to you to follow their example in committing your life to him?

3. MY LIFE SINCE I ENCOUNTERED CHRIST

- What difference has becoming a Christian made to you?
- What are the benefits?
- What has been the cost?
- What are your ongoing struggles?
- From your experience, why would you encourage others to turn to Christ?
- Write down your most recent transformation story.

Remember that, for many, this section will prove crucial. The 'proof of the pudding' will be in the living. What authenticates a genuine believer is not so much the 'sinner's prayer' but the 'saint's life'.

Don't forget that you're unlikely to need to share the whole of your story at any one time. We must always try to feed people according to their needs – that which is relevant to them at their stage in life. Imagine giving them a segment or two of an orange, not the whole thing. Provoke their curiosity and stimulate their interest, leaving them wanting more. Remember, the most effective evangelism is when the seeker is on the *offensive* ('sorry to bother you, but please tell me why . . .') and the Christian is on the *defensive* ('no that's perfectly OK – I'm happy to tell you why . . .'). The least effective is the other way round. Ensure you stop speaking before they stop listening, then there is the likelihood they will come back for more.

GUIDELINES TO HELP YOU PREPARE YOUR STORY
Pray first

The book of James says, 'If any of you lacks wisdom, you should ask God, who gives generously to all' (James 1:5).

Write it down

It says in 1 Peter 3:15, 'Always be prepared to give an answer to everyone who asks you . . .' Don't write pages and pages. Instead, keep it short so that you can remember it easily. Commit the points to memory – a rough-and-ready witness from the heart will be more effective than a stilted and polished performance.

Write out two versions: a 3-minute version and a 10-minute version. Edit out any theological language or religious jargon.

Ask a Christian friend to read it through and ask them if it is clear and true to the person they know you to be. You might also want to ask a friend who is not yet a follower of Jesus to read it for their comments.

Read it aloud to yourself until you are thoroughly familiar with it.

Be gentle and respect the person you're talking to

That same verse in Peter goes on to say, 'But do this with gentleness and respect.'

Avoid negative remarks about other religions and denominations. We don't ever need to put other religions down in order to lift Jesus up. (Of course, if people ask you about other religions, try to help them, constructively, to see where the Christian faith differs and what that might mean for them.)

We show respect by listening carefully to what they say and by observing and interpreting their body language.

Share, don't preach

Unlike in a sermon, you are sharing your experience. Remember you are the 'witness' not the 'lawyer'. Make it shamelessly experiential. Genuine sharing requires us to be honest, vulnerable and open to the responses that our story may evoke. God is not glorified by exaggeration or selective truth-telling. What we say must ring true.

Make use of the Bible

'For the word of God,' Hebrews 4:12 says, 'is alive and active. Sharper than any double-edged sword.' However, don't be a Bible-basher! Once again, feed people according to their needs, not according to how much Scripture you can stuff down their throats! Sometimes it is preferable to base what you have to say on just one verse or passage of the gospel. You might want to keep a few copies of the New Testament to give away after having shared a verse or story, leaving a marker in the page.

Make it real

Don't be tempted to hype it up or be embarrassed by a seemingly undramatic conversion story. Tell it as it is and God will use it. Remember, your story may seem ordinary to you because it is so familiar, but it may be strikingly fresh to the person with whom you are sharing.

Don't lapse into religious clichés

We all tend to speak in Christian jargon from time to time, but remember that people who haven't been to church won't know what you're talking about if you do. We have to keep it simple. In 1 Corinthians 2:1 Paul says, 'When I came to you, I did not come with eloquence or human wisdom as I proclaimed to you the testimony about God.'

Think for a moment about accessible language and how you might paraphrase terms like salvation, redemption, grace, sin and being born again.

Make it Christ-centred

Does your story give glory to Christ? Remember, Christ is the King of kings – you need to use your story to point to him. Inevitably, your testimony focuses on your experience but it must always point away from you to the Lord Jesus, who makes it all possible.

Keep it short and to the point

You're not preaching a sermon at church; you're sharing your story – the kind of story you just can't help sharing with others.

Writing it out provides a helpful discipline for you to review what you are saying. Revisit it from time to time to ensure that it is still current and to check whether it expresses your deepening understanding of the gospel.

A PRAYER

Lord Jesus Christ, thank you that you came to live among us, to bring God's story. Thank you that as our story intersects with your story we find ourselves in eternal history. We offer our stories to you and ask that you would help us to communicate them effectively to those around us – understanding that it is our lives that are the living, breathing evidence of the Good News of the kingdom of God. We also pray for everyone who will hear the story in the weeks, months and years to come and we ask that you would go before us to prepare them for what we have to say. In your name. Amen.

5

DEMONSTRATING
THE GOOD NEWS

SOCIAL JUSTICE AND EVANGELISM

WHO IS MY NEIGHBOUR?

A few years ago I visited Kenya with the charity Compassion. During the trip we visited Kiberia, a slum township outside Nairobi with a population of over half a million. Kiberia has no proper roads, no sewage system, no running water or electricity. The slum is entrenched in poverty, HIV is rampant and there is widespread unemployment. All the above conditions have meant that the township is particularly conducive to the spread of disease.

During the visit someone commented that these conditions would not be tolerated if this were a suburb of London, so why do we tolerate it merely because of the separation of miles? Such situations bring into sharp focus the question that the parable of the Good Samaritan would prompt us to ask: 'Who is my neighbour?'

In Luke 10:25–37 we read the parable of the Good Samaritan.

> An expert in the law stood up to test Jesus. 'Teacher,' he asked, 'what must I do to inherit eternal life?'
>
> 'What is written in the Law?' he replied. 'How do you read it?'
>
> He answered, '"Love the Lord your God with all your heart and with all your soul and with all your strength and with all your mind";

and, "Love your neighbour as yourself."'

'You have answered correctly,' Jesus replied. 'Do this and you will live.'

But he wanted to justify himself, so he asked Jesus, 'And who is my neighbour?'

In reply Jesus said: 'A man was going down from Jerusalem to Jericho, when he was attacked by robbers. They stripped him of his clothes, beat him and went away, leaving him half-dead. A priest happened to be going down the same road, and when he saw the man, he passed by on the other side. So too, a Levite, when he came to the place and saw him, passed by on the other side. But a Samaritan, as he travelled, came where the man was; and when he saw him, he took pity on him. He went to him and bandaged his wounds, pouring on oil and wine. Then he put the man on his own donkey, brought him to an inn and took care of him. The next day he took out two denarii and gave them to the innkeeper. "Look after him," he said, "and when I return, I will reimburse you for any extra expense you may have."

'Which of these three do you think was a neighbour to the man who fell into the hands of robbers?'

The expert in the law replied, 'The one who had mercy on him.'

Jesus told him, 'Go and do likewise.'

In this chapter we will focus on social justice and evangelism. There is a tendency to split the two in our minds into separate compartments. However, as we shall see, biblically both belong together. The demonstration and proclamation of the gospel are two sides of the same coin. We must resist the temptation to separate gospel words from gospel works. Editions of the New Testament that print the words of Christ in red may tempt us to do this!

Social justice, like evangelism, isn't something we can leave to the so-called 'experts'. And that's because it is, in fact, a fundamental part of the Good News of Jesus Christ – which we all have the responsibility of sharing. Social justice is embedded in the very message itself. God is on the side of those who have no one else to help them. And so our words must always be matched by our actions. Remember, we are not only to *speak* the Good News; we are to *be* the Good News. We must never allow a separation between lip and life, between proclamation and demonstration. We cannot be authentic disciples of Jesus if we fail to show the compassion of Jesus.

It is true that some within the Church will have a particular calling to either the demonstration or proclamation of the gospel and this will find expression in passion and gifting.

But this is not a licence to let the rest of us off the hook. Such people are to be 'prophetic irritants' in the body of Christ, provoking each one of us to play our part. In Matthew 25:37–40 Jesus said:

> Then the righteous will answer him, 'Lord, when did we see you hungry and feed you, or thirsty and give you something to drink? When did we see you a stranger and invite you in, or needing clothes and clothe you? When did we see you ill or in prison and go to visit you?'

The King will reply, 'Truly I tell you, whatever you did for one of the least of these . . . you did for me.'

As Christians, we are called to struggle against everything that condemns people to a sub-human existence – such as hunger, disease, poverty, inequality, exploitation, abuse and injustice. The struggle itself tells a story about the God we serve.

When the BBC presented a series based on a popular survey *The 100 Greatest Britons*, it was interesting to note which Christians made it onto the list: John Wesley, William Wilberforce, William Booth and Florence Nightingale.

Also, when an international research organisation carried out a worldwide survey on 'leaders who made a difference and whom you could not ignore', Mother Teresa came first and Archbishop Desmond Tutu second. All these people were characterised and compelled by a faith in Christ that was demonstrated in social action. Compassion and justice is a language the world understands and is deeply evangelistic. People can argue against proclamation, but cannot ignore a demonstration of the love of God.

THE BIBLE AND THE POOR

Jesus said, 'Blessed are you who are poor.' But what do we mean when we speak of 'the poor' today? Who and where are they?

We read in Deuteronomy 15:4–5,7–11 (NLT):

> There should be no poor among you, for the LORD your God will greatly bless you in the land he is giving you as a special possession. You will receive this blessing if you are careful to obey all the commands of the LORD your God that I am giving you today . . . But if there are any poor Israelites in your towns when you arrive in the land the LORD your God is giving you, do not be hard-hearted or tightfisted toward them. Instead, be generous and lend them whatever they need. Do not be mean-spirited and refuse someone a loan because the year for canceling debts is close at hand. If you refuse to make the loan and the needy person cries out to the LORD, you will be considered guilty of sin. Give

generously to the poor, not grudgingly, for the Lord your God will bless you in everything you do. There will always be some in the land who are poor. That is why I am commanding you to share freely with the poor and with other Israelites in need.

To the extent that this 'year of cancelling debts' was practised by Israel, it would provide a challenge and inspiration to the world at large. Unfortunately, there is no evidence of this 'setting things straight' once every 50 years being implemented in ancient Israel.

It's easy to see poverty as a self-inflicted wound – as something that the poor could have avoided through a bit more effort, some better management and a bit more luck. In our economic system, we've become used to the idea that the talented and hard-working people are duly rewarded, while the unlucky and the lazy ones also get what they deserve – nothing. But that's not how the Bible sees it.

It may feel as if the poor have always been around, but that is not the case. In fact, the book of Genesis doesn't mention the word 'poor' at all. It wasn't part of the original plan or indeed the natural order. In Abraham's time, if one person was rich, the whole tribe was rich – because wealth belonged to the tribe, not the individual.

Sadly, the sharing spirit didn't last forever. As the world 'developed', some became richer while others grew poorer. The story of God's involvement in human history – that starts in the Old Testament and proceeds into the New – is saturated with references to the poor. God clearly cares deeply about the fact that some have more than enough, while others have nothing. The advance of his kingdom is intrinsically linked with the liberation and salvation of the poor from their practical 'captivity', as much as any spiritual bondage. The world has enough for everyone's 'need' but not everyone's 'greed'.

In Jesus' day, poverty was widespread due to the crushing burden of taxation imposed by the Romans. People fled their homes when it became known that the tax gatherer was in the area. Subsistence farming meant that people not only faced starvation but also economic ruin when their harvests failed.

WHAT DOES THE BIBLE SAY?

The Old Testament uses several different words to describe 'the poor'. '*Ani*' is the most common word for 'poor' (occurring 77 times). It means 'a person who is bowed down'. The '*ani*' have to look up to others on whom they're dependent – contrasted, not as you might expect, with the 'rich' but with the 'oppressor', who keeps them in their place. '*Anaw*' is used 18 times and refers to people who feel they have little worth before God. The word '*ebyon*', meanwhile, is used 60 times to refer to the situation of beggars.

These three words are charged with emotion – they're not neutral or simply descriptive. All of them are a call for urgent change. When we think about the poor, let's be careful not to lump everyone into the same generic category. Hopefully, this biblical distinction helps us to think more compassionately about people who have little – and more critically of those of us who maintain the status quo (even if it's just through our own inactivity).

One role the Church can have is to challenge this 'status quo' – but when we do, let's not expect popularity. The South American Roman Catholic Bishop Hélder Câmara once said, 'When I feed the hungry they call me a saint – when I ask "Why are they hungry?" they call me a communist.'

The New Testament continues to record God's compassion for the poor with many references to the social conditions of the time. We read about landowners, tax collectors, labourers, slaves, honest and dishonest stewards, unjust judges and widows who plead for their rights.

The Bible doesn't just describe poverty in terms of money, but in terms of power. The most common Greek word for 'poor' in the New Testament is 'ptochos', which means 'to duck away in fear'. But the Bible suggests that God – the all-powerful – took upon himself 'the very nature of a servant' (Philippians 2:7), in order to turn the power structures of the world upside down and show us a better way – a way of justice, which brings peace and casts out all fear.

'Justice' is the opposite of 'just us'; it should never be 'just us'. To be a Christian is to become open to the rest of the world, not as a master but as a servant.

It's not that the poor are necessarily good people or that the rich are specifically evil. God is on the side of the poor *because no one else is.* And that means that we should be on their side too. In all of our relationships, we can choose to maintain power or to help to break it down; to maintain oppressive systems or to end them; to maintain the status quo (which serves us very nicely, thank you) or to fight for those who will otherwise for ever be without power, food, money and possibilities.

A PRAYER

God our Father, thank you for sending your Son to live with us and to show us how to live. Please help us to understand that the Good News is not just words, but also words in action – the practical outpouring of your love to anyone who needs it. Please give us the courage and strength to begin to change, if not the whole world, then the world around us. Amen.

ACTIONS SPEAK LOUDER THAN WORDS

Sometimes the most important things we *say* are the things that we *do* for people, such as being concerned about the concerns of others, loving and caring for those who are different to us and helping the marginalised and powerless. It is in doing these things that we become true witnesses and Natural Evangelists.

Social justice can go before evangelism in the sense that it can open closed doors, break down prejudice and become a bridge over which the gospel can pass. It has been said that people don't care how much we know, until they know how much we care.

However, we do not engage in social action as a means to evangelism, because that would introduce an ulterior motive or even make the help conditional on the person's eventual acceptance of the gospel. Loving acts are unconditional, neither demanding nor expecting anything in return.

Yet even if we don't manage to create that bridge, we must act with a social conscience regardless for, as Titus writes (2:14), one of the reasons Christ gave himself for us was 'to purify for himself a people that are his very own, eager to do what is good'.

Put another way, the book of James (2:14, NLT) says, 'What good is it, dear brothers and sisters, if you say you have faith but don't show it by your actions? Can that kind of faith save anyone?'

It isn't enough either just to have faith or, as budding evangelists, just to talk about faith; for (as James writes in James 2:17) 'faith by itself, if it is not accompanied by action, is dead'.

The Good News of Christ is that hope has broken into our hopeless world – this has radical and practical implications for us all. Faith in Christ entails exercising trust in him on a daily basis in every area of life. If we are not prepared to trust him in this way, then we are in no position to encourage others to put their faith in Christ.

What are we already doing – as individuals, as a home-group, as a church – to ensure that our faith finds expression in social justice? Contemplate opportunities for doing more. Don't dismiss an idea on whether it's good or whether it's practical or not. Every idea is a possibility.

We should never separate words, works and wonders. After all, there is no competition between lighthouse keepers and lifeboat savers.

And we must not forget that those things we do *for* God we must also do *with* God. Mother Teresa once said of her work in Calcutta:

> We try to pray through our work by doing it with Jesus, for Jesus, to Jesus. That helps us to put our whole heart and soul into doing it. The dying, the crippled, the mentally ill, the unwanted, the unloved – they are Jesus in disguise.

As we contemplate ways in which we can demonstrate the gospel, it is easy to be overwhelmed by the enormous need all around us. Consider the story of the couple walking along a beach throwing stranded starfish back into the sea. A passer-by commented on the futility of their actions: 'What difference are you making? There are thousands of starfish on this beach alone.' One of the couple responded, with starfish in hand, 'It means everything to this one.'

We've much to do and little time to do it. No one person can change the world, but we can all change the world for one person. And that's an amazing possibility and privilege. As the eighteenth-century philosopher Edmund Burke wrote, 'Nobody made a greater mistake than he who did nothing because he could only do a little.'

Archbishop Desmond Tutu gave this advice to an enquirer who was faced with the temptation of the paralysis of analysis: 'How do you eat an elephant? . . . One chunk at a time!' When it comes to our committee deliberations, we often have to confess that when all is said and done, a lot more is said than done!

We returned from our Compassion trip to Kenya both shocked and stirred, but also encouraged to see how Compassion's child-sponsorship programme has transformed the lives of thousands. One highlight from the trip was having a meal with four university students who were living in slums when Compassion rescued them. We heard incredible testimonies of how Compassion had helped transform their lives.

Why not prayerfully consider sponsoring a child with Compassion. (For further information, see Appendix 2.)

The prayer of St Francis of Assisi seems so appropriate:

A PRAYER
Lord, make us instruments of your peace.
Where there is hatred, let us sow love;
Where there is injury, pardon;
Where there is discord, union;
Where there is doubt, faith;
Where there is despair, hope;

Where there is darkness, light;
Where there is sadness, joy.
Grant that we may not so much seek to be consoled
  as to console;
To be understood as to understand;
To be loved as to love.
For it is in giving that we receive;
It is in pardoning that we are pardoned;
And it is in dying that we are born to eternal life.
Amen.

6

HOW CAN WE BE
EMPOWERED FOR EVANGELISM?

POWER FOR A PURPOSE

In this final chapter we will ask, 'How can we receive power for evangelism?'

The exciting and fascinating story written by Luke in the book of Acts records how the disciples powerfully received the Holy Spirit. It's about real people in a real-life situation, like you and me today. Luke's message is simply this: the Spirit of God is doing *his* thing in the midst of a world intent on doing *its* thing. He records the acts of the Holy Spirit through the Acts of the Apostles.

The word 'Pentecost' literally means 'fiftieth'. When God sent his Spirit upon the disciples in the upper room, it was the fiftieth day after Passover (the annual celebration of that great moment in Israel's history when they were delivered by God from captivity in Egypt). The disciples received power, which took them out onto the streets of Jerusalem to spread the Good News, and then way beyond . . .

The book of Acts goes on to record the story of what followed; it is jam-packed with both talk and action. There are riots, demonstrations, arrests, shipwreck, humour . . . all of which is, in fact, incidental to the real action that threads its way throughout these events.

And that golden thread is evangelism – the Good News of Jesus Christ. Purely and simply, Acts is about spreading this Good News and about how we must depend on the power of the Spirit to make the news real and relevant to all who hear it.

The question is, 'What can we learn from the activity of the Holy Spirit in the book of Acts?' Jesus promised, 'You will receive power when the Holy Spirit comes on you' (Acts 1:8). In this chapter, we will explore what that means for the earliest followers of Jesus, and for those of us today who follow in their footsteps.

In Acts 2:1–4 (NLT) we read:

> On the day of Pentecost all the believers were meeting together in one place. Suddenly, there was a sound from heaven like the roaring of a mighty windstorm, and it filled the house where they were sitting. Then, what looked like flames or tongues of fire appeared and settled on each of them. And everyone present was filled with the Holy Spirit and began speaking in other languages, as the Holy Spirit gave them this ability.

Jesus promises in Acts 1:8 that 'you will receive power when the Holy Spirit comes on you'. But why? Pentecost is not only about God's saving grace, bringing the application of salvation to our lives; nor is it simply an ethical event, designed to help transform our character. It is also *missiological*, propelling us to share the Good News of Christ.

This is why Jesus continues the statement, saying, 'you will be my witnesses in Jerusalem, and in all Judea and Samaria, and to the ends of the earth' (Acts 1:8).

In the New Testament, there is a connection between being *filled up, charged up* and *sent out.*

God empowers us for a purpose. God's Holy Spirit not only helps us to know Christ, but also helps us to make Christ known.

FIRST FRUITS

Pentecost was also called the Feast of the First Fruits; it was the time at which the first ripe corn was offered to God. And in Acts 2, we see the 'first fruits' of the harvest of the gospel – a harvest that is still being gathered all over the world today.

So when the Spirit came at Pentecost they all became witnesses! The Spirit is the moving power, energy, inspiration and strength behind *all* evangelism.

The Holy Spirit guides us and equips us. And the Holy Spirit alone can bring conviction and faith to people who don't know Jesus. Our part is to be the messenger. So without the Spirit we labour in vain.

SIX WAYS THE SPIRIT HELPS US

1. BY CALLING US TO BE A MISSIONARY

What me? A missionary? That's right! From a New Testament perspective, all Christians are called to be missionaries. The question is, 'In what capacity am I called?' Remember, a missionary is not a person who crosses the sea, but a person who sees the cross. When you have seen the cross, the love of Christ compels you.

The book of Acts provides us with two spheres or capacities for being a missionary and the good news is that the Holy Spirit helps us to discern which we are called to be.

First, there are the *'workplace'* missionaries, for example the apostles who remained in Jerusalem after Pentecost (Acts 8:1). For most Christians, their primary missionary sphere is their place of work. Remember that the *household* in the New Testament was a place of business and social contact.

Second, there are *'wandering'* missionaries like Paul, Barnabas and Philip (Acts 8:4). These tend to be Christians who have a primary gifting in evangelism, preaching and teaching the gospel. These would also include itinerant evangelists (like me) and cross-cultural mission partners.

We need both types of missionaries in today's world. And as we try to discern which type we might be, the Holy Spirit will help to guide us; the Spirit is the driving force behind all of our evangelism.

2. PRAYER

Prayer is crucial if we wish to evangelise effectively. It is oxygen for the holy fire. The New Testament itself is soaked in references to prayer. In fact, it knows no evangelism without prayer, and no prayer that does not lead to evangelism. Luke, in his Gospel, relates everything to prayer – not that prayer is everything but, rather, that everything is prayer.

Jesus is our ultimate model and Jesus always prayed before he acted. 'The harvest is plentiful,' he said in Matthew 9:37–38, 'but the workers are few. Ask the Lord of the harvest, therefore, to send out workers into his harvest field.'

In the upper room, while Jesus was with his disciples partaking in the Last Supper, his longest recorded prayer is found. He prayed for himself and for the completion of his own mission.

Then he prayed for his disciples, 'As you sent me into the world, I have sent them into the world' (John 17:18). And then Jesus prays for all who will believe in him through their message.

His prayer life motivated others to pray. We read that, in that famous upper room in Jerusalem, the disciples 'all joined together constantly in prayer, along with the women and Mary the mother of Jesus, and with his brothers' (Acts 1:14).

As John Wesley said, 'God does nothing but in answer to prayer.' It's not just that prayer can launch a spiritual awakening; prayer can turn out to *be* the awakening itself. And today, churches that experience revival are those that are characterised by prayer.

If we want to work for God, we should form a committee – but God so loved the world that he did not send a committee! However, if we want to work *with* God, we should pray. As the apostle Paul wrote, 'I urge you . . . by our Lord Jesus Christ and by the love of the Spirit, to join me in my struggle by praying to God for me' (Romans 15:30).

We should pray because we cannot achieve anything through clever plans alone, but through the work of the Holy Spirit. It is crucial that we mobilise prayer in order to evangelise, for prayer is one of the spiritual weapons God has given us. Unused weapons do not win wars.

When we pray, we get involved in missionary work. But it's important that we try to see prayer not just as something we do on Sundays at church or Wednesday nights at a home-group, but to see it as a way of life, as something that permeates and infuses our journey.

What should be the content of our prayers?

The Bible calls us to pray more for those who are conveying the Good News of Jesus Christ than those who are receiving it. This is because conversion is ultimately the work of the Holy Spirit. It is the messengers who need God's help.

We are instructed to pray into five basic areas:

1. Pioneers: for workers to be sent to the mission field (Matthew 9:38).

2. Planning: for guidance – for who to send and where to go (Acts 13:2–3).

3. Productivity: for the success of the message (Acts 4:29–31).

4. Protection: for protection and help for missionaries and all who witness (Psalm 5:11).

5. Persecutors: for our enemies and persecutors. Jesus leads the way by asking his Father to forgive those who are crucifying him (Luke 23:34).

And what form should they take?

Prayer can take many different forms. It doesn't just have to be a set of written or spoken words. As you try to make prayer a way of life, think creatively about how you can pray in different ways and at different times. I like to walk and pray. Others enjoy using the arts as a means of praying.

Take a moment to reflect on your church and personal prayer life.

- Can any changes and improvements be made to develop your prayer life in relation to evangelism?

- Can you pray in different ways?

3. THE SPIRIT HELPS US IN PERSONAL EVANGELISM

As we try to spread the Good News of Christ to others, it's important to remain attuned to the Holy Spirit, who not only brings us power and confidence, but also guidance.

Sometimes God can ask us to perform a specific task. In Acts 8:26–40, we read the story of Philip and the Ethiopian eunuch. Philip acts on the prompting he gets to go and run alongside the chariot of the Ethiopian. From there, he is able to take the opportunity God has given, to speak the Good News to this man.

The Holy Spirit will sometimes guide us in a similar way. Our responsibility is to listen for his promptings, and then – just as importantly – to act upon them. Think carefully, however, about the way you go about this. If you believe that God is telling you to pray for someone's healing, ask them if you can pray for them. But don't tie yourself – or God – down by saying that God is going to heal them. Allow God to work through you and act in obedience to his still, small voice. God answers prayers in different ways at different times – the secret is to never stop praying.

4. THE SPIRIT GIVES DIRECTION
IN CHURCH EVANGELISM

In Acts 16, Paul and his team experience all sorts of frustrations. Doors seem to be closing in their faces rather than opening. Their plans seem to be thwarted at every turn. But it turns out to be the work of the Holy Spirit.

They had to learn to 'die' to their own plans for the sake of God's plans; to die to their own timetable, in order to live by God's. And when they do (Acts 17 – 20), we see God opening up an amazing new door into Europe for them.

The Lord may shut doors before he guides us to the one he has opened. It is not that we shouldn't make our own plans and be creative and diligent about how we try to spread the gospel; God wants us to take the initiative. But sometimes he has a different plan, so we must be patient and sensitive to the calling of the Holy Spirit as we pursue the path he wants us to travel.

For example, a number of churches have discovered that certain areas of their local communities are more receptive to the gospel than others. Clearly, this doesn't mean that we don't keep trying in the tougher, barren areas, but it does mean we should pray about where God wants us to focus our efforts. It might be in one place or group in particular, such as children, the elderly, single parents, and so on . . .

When the Spirit is moving, expect and prepare for new life to spring up.

THINK ABOUT

Think about your own locality and the area your church seeks to serve.

- Where has the gospel been received effectively and enthusiastically?

- Where has it fallen on hard ground?

Spend a few quiet minutes listening to God to see if he is directing your thoughts towards any region or area in particular. If you sense strongly that God is directing you, make a note, and let your church leadership know.

5. THE SPIRIT HELPS US TO WITNESS THROUGH WORD, WORKS AND WONDERS

In our last chapter, we saw how God empowers us to communicate his love through works as well as word; social action as well as proclamation. The third 'w' is 'wonders'.

The first Christians regularly saw healing and 'deliverance' as part of their evangelism. When Jesus sent out his mission teams, 'he gave them power and authority to drive out all demons and to cure diseases, and he sent them out to proclaim the kingdom of God and to heal those who were ill' (Luke 9:1–2).

It was only natural, therefore, that the disciples should do the same. They were, after all, following in his footsteps. In Acts 3:1–10 and Acts 19:11–16, we see that God loves the world so much that he wants to bring healing and deliverance from all kinds of bondage.

I believe we should seek insight and wisdom from God to be prophetic in our evangelism. As I have sought God as to how I should pray for a person who is sick, or speak to someone who is not yet a Christian, the Lord has given me insight and wisdom to know how to pray or speak a word into someone's life that dramatically transforms them.

6. THE SPIRIT HELPS US TO UNDERSTAND SPIRITUAL WARFARE

We often look at the world and think that there is little we can do to change it. But the Holy Spirit helps us to see the way God sees. That changes everything.

In the Old Testament, the prophet Joel prophesied that God would pour his Spirit out upon all people and that this outpouring would be characterised by a release of prophecy and vision. In other words, God would help us to see things from heaven's point of view.

This involves acknowledging that there are what we call 'principalities and powers' at work (Ephesians 6:12); forces which are trying to bring evil to reign and to thwart our attempts to spread the Good News across the world.

It is important that we discern the strategies of the devil and his demonic army. Satan even ended up thwarting the apostle Paul at times (see 1 Thessalonians 2:18) – so we should not be surprised if we encounter such resistance.

This is not to say we should be afraid or focus unduly on the power of Satan. Paul reminds us to 'put on the full armour of God, so that when the day of evil comes, you may be able to stand your ground' (Ephesians 6:13).

We can put on the belt of truth, the breastplate of righteousness and have 'feet fitted with the readiness that comes from the gospel of peace'. There's also the shield of faith and the helmet of salvation. It is important that we put on this armour, day by day. Perhaps when you are getting dressed in the morning, try to think of putting on this additional spiritual armour.

In Ephesians 6:10–18 (NLT) we read:

A final word: Be strong in the Lord and in his mighty power. Put on all of God's armor so that you will be able to stand firm against all strategies of the devil. For we are not fighting against flesh-and-blood enemies, but against evil rulers and authorities of the unseen world, against mighty powers in this dark world, and against evil spirits in the heavenly places.

Therefore, put on every piece of God's armor so you will be able to resist the enemy in the time of evil. Then after the battle you will still be standing firm. Stand your ground, putting on the belt of truth and the body armor of God's righteousness. For shoes, put on the peace that comes from the Good News so that you will be fully prepared. In addition to all of these, hold up the shield of faith to stop the fiery arrows of the devil. Put on salvation as your helmet, and take the sword of the Spirit, which is the word of God.

Pray in the Spirit at all times and on every occasion. Stay alert and be persistent in your prayers for all believers everywhere.

Paul instructs us to put on 'the full armour of God'. Have a look at the list below. Are there any pieces that you are prone to overlook? What have been the consequences? Resolve not to overlook them in the future.

- Belt of Truth
- Breastplate of Righteousness
- Shoes of the Gospel of Peace
- Shield of Faith
- Helmet of Salvation
- Sword of the Spirit

CONCLUDING REMARKS

The book of Acts (written by Luke) is all about spreading the Good News of Jesus Christ. It does not, however, sanction any one method. The apostles used every way they could think of to get the word out. The only model is 'saturation' evangelism. We must be open to any ideas, and to new ideas, as we seek to express the transforming Good News of Christ to a dying world.

We may be 'only' human, but thankfully we have the power of God to help us in our adventure. We can speak the Good News of Christ in the power of the Holy Spirit, so that Jesus is revealed in our own time and in our own place. *The main thing is to keep the main thing the main thing*: to know Christ, and to make Christ known.

I would like to draw this book to a close with these moving words from my friend Dr Leighton Ford:

> Jesus was born in a borrowed manger. He preached from a borrowed boat. He entered Jerusalem on a borrowed donkey. He ate the Last Supper in a borrowed upper room and he was buried in a borrowed tomb. Now he asks to borrow the lives of his followers to reach the rest of the world. If we do not speak, then he is dumb and silent.

To conclude this book and to commission you to go out, I would like you to read this prayer. After you have done so, pray for the Holy Spirit to fill you up and send you out in power.

A PRAYER

by J.H. Jowett

Grant that we may walk as Christ walked.
Grant that what Spirit was in him,
such he may be also in us.
Grant that our lives may be re-fashioned
after the pattern of his life.
Grant that we may do today here on earth,
what Christ would have done,
and in the way he would have done it.
Grant that we may become vessels of his grace,
instruments of his will –
to thy honour and glory.
Through Jesus Christ our Lord. Amen.

FINAL WORD

This book has taken you on a journey. I hope you have learned that we are all called to the work of evangelism, that we are all called to spread the Good News of Christ and that we all do so only in the power of the Spirit of God. We are not alone. God has walked the path before us and has sent his Spirit to live in us and empower us – that for the sake of the King and the Kingdom, we may truly know Christ and make Christ known.

APPENDIX 1

BIBLE REFERENCES FROM CHAPTER 1

Creation

Genesis 1:1–4; John 1:1–3; Acts 17:24–26;
Colossians 1:15–16

Chaos

Genesis 3:22–24; Isaiah 53:5–6; Romans 3:23; Romans 5:12

Covenant

Genesis 9:8–11; Genesis 15:18 – 21:1; Exodus 19:3–6;
Jeremiah 31:31–34

Christ the Mediator

Mark 14:22–25; 2 Corinthians 5:18–19; Ephesians 2:14–18;
Colossians 1:19–20; 1 Timothy 2:5–6; Hebrews 9:13–15;
1 Peter 3:18

Christ the Conqueror

Luke 24:1–8; 1 Corinthians 15:21–28;
1 Corinthians 15:54–57

Certainty

Matthew 24:13–14; Romans 8:15–17; Galatians 4:6–7;
Ephesians 1:13–14; 1 John 2:3–6

APPENDIX 2

ORGANISATIONS QUOTED

Compassion UK

Compassion is an international Christian child development and advocacy ministry. Partnering with local churches, Compassion is committed to the spiritual, economic, social and physical development of children living in extreme poverty, enabling them to become responsible, fulfilled Christian adults.

For more information, see: www.compassionuk.org

Compassion UK
43 High Street
Weybridge
Surrey
KT13 8BB

Tel: 01932 836490
Fax: 01932 831275
E-mail: info@compassionuk.org